LITHUANIAN MYTHOLOGY & LEGENDS

Journey Through Time with Myths and Folklore

CHRONICLE PRESS

Copyright © 2023

All rights reserved. Without the showing prior written permission of the publisher, no portion of this book may be copied, kept in a retrieval system, or communicated in any form, whether mechanical, electronic, photocopying, recording or otherwise. This includes transmitting it in any language.

Copyright © 2023

Disclaimer

The author is solely responsible for this book's information, ideas, and opinions; they do not necessarily represent the views of any organizations, institutions, or individuals associated with the author. The author has made what they believe to be reasonable steps to make sure that the material contained in this book is accurate. However, neither the author nor the publisher makes any representations or guarantees, either stated or implied, regarding the completeness, accuracy, reliability, appropriateness, or availability of the content contained within. It is strongly recommended that readers seek assistance from relevant professionals or specialists in specific disciplines by consulting with them to acquire precise information tailored to their particular situations. The author disclaims liability for any loss, damage, or harm resulting from using the information provided in this book and any omissions or errors.

This book may reference websites, goods, services, or resources owned or operated by third parties. These references are solely offered for your convenience, and their inclusion does not indicate that we approve, sponsor, or recommend the content provided by the third party. Because the author and the publisher do not have any control over the nature, content, or availability of external websites, they cannot be held liable for any actions, decisions, or consequences resulting from using such external resources.

Forward

I would want to extend an invitation to go on a voyage that is genuinely extraordinary to those of you who are interested in unearthing ancient knowledge, who are captivated by the mysterious stories that are woven through the fabric of human life, and who are aficionados of the rich tapestry of mythology that transcends boundaries and resonates across time. Within this book's covers, we will explore the halls of myth and completely submerge ourselves in the ageless tales that have enthralled the human imagination for as long as anybody can remember.

In all of its magnificence, mythology acts as a compass that directs us through the complexities of the human experience. It is a mirror that reflects our perception of the universe and our role and embodies our collective dreams, fears, goals, and ideals. Mythology invites us to investigate the hidden aspects of our lives, whether we are more interested in the sweeping conflicts between gods and heroes or the hidden meanings in the stories of how the world was created.

Within these pages, you will encounter many pantheons and deities, each providing a distinctive perspective to examine the more expansive universe. As we delve deeper into these enthralling tales, it is essential to remember that mythology is not only a relic of the past but a living phenomenon that continues to impact our contemporary reality. Its influence can be seen in literature, art, music, and daily language. It invigorates us, sparks the fire of our imagination, and gives us a glimpse into the intricate web that is the history of humanity.

Mythology also acts as a connector, bringing together people from different cultures worldwide. It brings us together by highlighting the similarities in our experiences and the uniqueness of each of us as individuals. In the vast Pantheon of mythical figures, we find examples of universal themes such as love, betrayal, heroism, and sacrifice. These themes connect with every human heart, regardless of when or where they were written.

This book is both a celebration of mythology and an invitation to go on an adventure of discovery. This is a homage to the innumerable storytellers who have ensured the survival of these myths through the ebb and flow of the sands of time by passing them down from generation to generation. It is devoted to all people interested in mythology, namely those who find comfort in the ageless stories that have shaped our world since the beginning of time and continue to do so today.

Therefore, I implore you, dear reader, to turn the page and completely submerge yourself in the enthralling delights that are still to come. Let us all come together to celebrate the mythology that brings us together, that is not limited by the constraints of culture or time, and imparts a feeling of awe and wonder into our everyday lives.

Your imagination will be stoked, your horizons will be expanded, and you will be reminded of the eternal power of storytelling if you allow yourself to go on this voyage into the realms of mythology. And may you emerge from these pages, like the heroes of old, changed by the insight and enchantment that mythology has to give due to what you've learned here.

TABLE OF CONTENTS

Forward

Chapter 1: Introduction

Chapter 2: Gods and Heros

Dievas: God of Sky

Perkūnas: God of thunder

Velnias: God of the Underworld

Chapter 3: Goddess

Veliona: Goddess of the dead

Goddess Gabija: Goddess of Fire

Chapter 4: Mythical Creatures

Zaltys: Household Spirit

Kaukas:Sprit of Harvest

Aitvaras: Guardian of Water

Chapter 5: Legends

The concept of the Life after Death

Neris and Nemunas

CHAPTER 1: INTRODUCTION

Lithuania's religion is one of the Baltic religions. It has many connections to the religions of Prussia and Latvia. Along with the traditional religions of Northern and Central Europe, it shows how Indo-European religions work. It stands out because of its social aspect: neither the Prussians nor the Lithuanians had formed a sovereign state by that time, and neither knighthood nor warriors had become solid social classes. On the other hand, sources from the thirteenth and fourteenth centuries usually talk about the religions that the soldiers and lords followed. In the thirteenth and fourteenth centuries, the military-aristocratic part of the Baltic state religions stood out because it comprised people from these social groups. In sources from the 15th and 16th centuries, as well as folklore and ethnography from the 19th and 20th centuries, we can see that peasants held firm beliefs. This may have been partly caused by the spread of Christianity among the influential people in society, who then lost their national identity. At the same time, the peasants slowly became Christians, and farming legends were revived for some years.

There is a vague mention in Tacitus' "Germania" of gentes aestiorum, which adore the Mother of Gods, and other sources that say they are from the Western Balts. Reports from the Arabic explorer Idrisius about people from Madsuna town who worship fire could also be from a source in Lithuania. There is much information about the Baltic groups in the cattle of popes and other sources. Ipatijus Voluinė's manuscript fragments give a better picture of Lithuanian religion. They talk about gods Mindaugas secretly worshipped, and gods Lithuanian warriors asked for help. There is also a short section in the Slavic translation of Malala's chronicle about Sovijus's myth, which is accurate but does not clearly explain its meaning. The documents from the Lyvonic and Teutonic Orders are from different sources. However, they are broken up and don't help protect the original material. There are more sources from before and right after Christianity was accepted. Even though they are romanticised, the data from Hieronymus Praquensis and Jan Dlugosz give us much information.

In later Renaissance sources, like late texts, stories about Lithuanian history come alive, some of which are religious. The "Lithuanian Chronicle" discusses religious changes in the early Middle Ages. Earlier records don't back up these changes, but the general religious changes in the Baltic show that they were real. In the latter part of the 1600s, Maciej Stryjkowski wrote a list of 16 Lithuanian gods. Later, J. Lasycki wrote a list of many Samogitian gods and some small mythological figures. Although these writers can be trusted, they weren't fluent in Lithuanian and were writing about a religion falling apart. This religion was filled with many locally worshipped "gods" and small mythical figures.

This mess doesn't lend itself to being put into a clear category. Towards the end of the sixteenth century and into the 17th century and later, there were a lot of Jesuit missions in Lithuania. Much information was passed along about the remains of the pagan religion that could be found in the Lithuanian region. M. Preatorius wrote regarding the traditions and customs in Lithuania Minor; his works are essential because they differ from the fragments discovered in earlier sources and are more like a complete ethnographic. When all of these pieces are put together, they can help reconstruct the Lithuanian tradition. However, it is essential to remember that these facts only show certain stages in the development of the Lithuanian religious tradition, including its peak and trough times. "Mechanical adding up" would not give a complete picture of the old Lithuanian religion. Another group of sources that could be added here are language and archaeological sources, folklore collections from the 19th and 20th centuries, and ethnographic stuff from the time. But we can guess that the answers to our question depend on how detailed the different sources are, and the order of the sources is also critical.

The 13th-century Russian texts talk about the gods that the Lithuanians believed in. The text that Ipatij wrote in 1252 about Mindaugas' baptism says that the royal baptism was fake and that Mindaugas kept giving gifts to his old gods, such as the chief Nunadievis, Teliavelis, Diviriks, the God of Hares, and Medina. People in Lithuania were praying to their gods, Andajus and Diviriks, around 1258. Sovijus made sacrifices to Andajus as well as Perkūnas, lightning, to ſvorūna, a dog whore, and Teliavelis, an ironworker who made the sun and raised it into the sky to light the earth. This story was translated by Jon Malala in 1261 and added to the original text. This gives a good overview of the Pantheon; you can trust it since the information comes from two reliable sources supporting each other.

The history of the country is fascinating. Most

people think that because Lithuania is in the north and has ties to the Soviet Union, it might be like Russia or Scandinavia. However, while some parts of these cultures have been closely linked for hundreds of years, the language spoken in Lithuania today has very little in common with Russian or Scandinavian. Instead, it comes from Sanskrit, which means it has Proto-Indo-European roots. Even though it had ties to other places, Lithuania was physically alone at the time and kept its pagan culture alive. It may sound strange to people who know little about the area's past. However, by the fourteenth century. It was almost as big as the Roman Empire and almost twice as big as modern-day France. Many different cultures and languages lived in the Duchy, which now includes parts of Poland, Ukraine, Russia, and Belarus. They were all connected by their belief in paganism. As a practice that was firmly rooted in Lithuanian culture, national beliefs, and farming methods, among other things, paganism was also a way to keep people from different countries close through religion. Lithuania was a pagan country for a long time because its rulers used their military power and diplomacy skills to maintain alliances, negotiate with Christians and avoid significant battles between the two groups.

Because of this time in history, Lithuania still follows its old customs. Anyone who goes to any market will see traditional goods like honey, mead, wreaths, and leather bags with "wiccan" symbols on them. You can often see these images in the background of Lithuania's 2023 Eurovision performance.

Let's learn more about religion's past in Lithuania now that the audience knows more about it. Of course, poly is just another word for polytheism, which is the belief in many gods and sometimes creatures and people from other worlds. I don't know what to call very early Baltic folklore, but East Prussia sources from the Middle Ages talk about Romuva and Romowe. It was thought that Romowe was a haven for witches. Its roots refer to Proto-Indo-European, meaning "quiet" or "sanctuary." It looked like many pagan people in Lithuania, and those who came after them tried to restore what was lost when the country became Christian. It is a new religion with a lot of links to Buddhism as well as Hinduism. They called it Romuva.

And, of course, every story has its gods, so let's take a quick look at the magical world of the Baltic gods. First, there is Perkūnas, who is like Thor and is the god of thunder. Along with Dievas, the most important god, he is one of the majority essential gods. Dievas is now what people in Lithuania call the Christian God. While Dievas is known as the "main god of the sky," Perkūnas was probably most important because so many stories, scripts, and customs were based on him. Much has been said and written about the hierarchy and system of the Baltic faiths. However, most people think it is set up like a pantheon of gods, with some of the most important ones being Saulė, the deity of the Sun, who is often pictured and worshipped; Mėnuo, the Moon; Laima, the goddess of destiny, and many others.

There are many folk tales besides old pagan gods. The two most important ones come from writings from the 1800s, but based on what I've read, it seems likely that earlier versions were passed down orally from one family to the next. There are stories about Elgė, the Queen of Serpents, and Jūratė, a Baltic version of the little mermaid. The people in these stories are linked to pagan mythology. Perkūnas breaks her amber house in the mermaid story when she realizes she likes a human. This is why, per the story, there is so much broken amber on the Lithuanian coast. The story of Elg× is more complicated and a little older, but only by about five years. The name comes from the word "spruce tree" and is common in Lithuania.

The story is very complicated, and there are many different versions of it. Still, the most well-known story in Lithuanian society is about how a snake got caught in Elgė's sleeve and only agreed to leave herself if she married him. Yes, she agrees. They have four kids together, and one day, they will ask Elg about her family. It makes her miss her parents, so she asks to see them. She can't do that until she uses magic to finish three impossible jobs that the Snake Prince sets for her. When she got home, her family missed her and decided to kill the Snake Prince, which they did. When Elgė finds out that her husband is deceased, she turns herself and her family into trees. She is a spruce, which is how she got her name.

CHAPTER 2: GODS AND HEROS

In mythology, gods are strong and often mystical beings important to different cultures' beliefs, stories, and customs. Most of the time, these divine beings are shown to have unique powers, like shaping the world, affecting natural events, and deciding people's fates. In different countries and times, gods represent different things, like wisdom, strength, love, and even mischief. They are the main characters in myths, legends, and religious stories.

People study the stories and tales about the gods to figure out their role in explaining the unidentified, teaching moral lessons, and keeping society in order. These stories give people hope, direction, and sometimes fear. In mythology, gods tell stories that explain human nature, the enigmas of life, and the complicated connections between people and the gods. This chapter discusses these gods' different areas and qualities, focusing on how they are connected to natural events, human feelings, and social norms. It provides a thorough and exciting look at the divine by breaking down the complicated stories of gods in mythology.

Dievas: God of Sky

Dievas or Dievs was the name of a sky god that people in the Baltic used to worship. Dievas' facial traits are not talked about in great detail. He was a young man who wore silver, felt, and satin clothes and carried a shiny silver-green sword resembling the ones Baltic dukes used to carry. He needed to put on a grey coat and a white shirt. He wore a veil sometimes so that people wouldn't think of him as a leader. At will, Dievas could change into an old man, and he went from house to residence and village to village, visiting people, giving them gifts and assisting them.

People thought that Dievas made gods, not as the one who made everything but as the one who made human culture. He was a god who made sure the world had rules and laws. Many people thought Dievas dwelt on his farm at the top of a tall, silver mountain. His farm was prosperous on earth. It had gardens, fields, houses, and a pirtis. Dievas possessed a golden or silver carriage or sleigh pulled by two spotted horses known as Dievo žirgai. These mounts sometimes looked like black dogs or blackbirds. Dievas rode with his horses, too. He rode down his mountain in heaven to make the fields more fertile. Slowly riding down from the mountain, he talked about how spring and summer were coming. His look changed with the sun's phases, and he had been closely linked to Saulė, the sun goddess. He is sometimes shown as her husband, brother, or close helper. During the fair of Rasa, which happened at the start of summer, both Dievas and Saulė were honoured.

Many people considered Dievas a horse goddess because she was closely linked to horses. The ancient Balts thought that horses were gifts from Dievas. He was considered a god who helped people who rode horses and advised them on how to raise and care for them. Dievas was also linked to Laima, the goddess of faith with three sides. Dievas is even Laima's biological father in some stories. It was said that Dievas could see births, weddings, and deaths because he was the god of traditional values and law and order. He was asked to participate in ceremonies where oaths and vows were made. People believed in both Laima and Dievas as gods. Many folk tales talk about fights and clashes between Dievas and Laima. Most of the time, she won the fights. In the latter part of the Middle Ages, when the Baltic lands became Christian, the name Dievas was picked to stand for the Christian god. It was because Dievas was a god loved and admired among the old Baltic people and was seen as one of the most important gods in the Baltic realm.

In many societies, the sky and thunder gods are the same person. However, in Baltic mythology, Dievas and Perkūnas are two separate characters. This island is called Perkūnas because it comes from the Proto-Baltic word Perk, which means oak. The name of this person is Pīrkons in Latvian and Perkuns in Prussian. One old Finnish name for Ukko, the thunder god, was Perkele. Fire, thunder, order, and chaos were all controlled by Pērkons. Perkūnas had holy lands all over Lithuania. They were called Alkos. In these woods, sacred fires were kept going to keep the Perkūnas safe. The women who watched over the fire wore vestals. People thought that hills and trees that had been "touched" by Perkūnas lightning were holy. If Perkūnas hit a tree or rock, it would protect you from evil and sickness.

To the people of Lithuania, Dievas is the god who represents the sky, light, peace, and friendship. He is the one who makes plants grow. He has small birds, horses, stags, and bulls as pets. Birches, ryes, and other trees that lose their leaves in the fall are holy to him. He is also the one who made the Lithuanian sagas. His job is to reward good individuals as well as punish hunks. Dievas is sometimes like Dievas Senelis, yet he is also very clever. In one story, Dievas washed his face with water when a dirty drop fell to the ground and turned into a person. Dievas and his brother Velnias go places together a lot. Velnias always tries to be like Dievas or get in the way of her, but his work turns terrible and gets stuck.

People say that Dievas made the ground. He told Velnias to dig up some dirt at the bottom for the ocean of the deep. Velnias dove several times, but water washed the dirt off his hands each time. Then Dievas saw dirt in Velnias' nails. Dievas used the dirt to make a seed and then threw it into the pool of water. The seed turned into a little dirt. Velnias and Dievas stayed the night together on the bit. While Dievas was sleeping, Velnias cursed him and wanted to kill him. He grabbed Dievas and dragged him into the water. The ground grew where Dievas flew.

Perkūnas: God of thunder

He is the creator of weather, lightning, and thunder. Perkūnas stands for the creative forces, bravery, success, the sky, rainfall, thunder, heavenly fire, and the elements of the sky. Potrimpo represents the seas, the ground, crops, and grains, and Velnias or Patulas represent hell and death. In his role as a god in heaven, Perkūnas seems to help Dievas carry out her will. However, Perkūnas is more critical than Dievas, the otiosus god, since he can be seen and has clear mythological roles. It shows Perkūnas as a middle-aged man with an axe and arrows who rides a two-wheeled carriage pulled by goats, similar to Thor or the Celtic god Taranis. Other stories say that the thunder god rides a fiery horse or drives a fiery carriage through the sky on fast horses.

There are songs regarding a "heavenly wedding" where Saul cheats in Perkūnas with Mėnulis. With a sword, Perknas cuts Mėnulis in half. Another more common story says that Mėnulis cheats in the Sun with Aušrinė right after their marriage, and Perkūnas punishes her for it. It doesn't learn; it cheats every month, getting punished again. Some say this is why the Sunbeams during the day or the Moon shines at night. They are no longer married but desire to see their little girl, Emina. Perkūnas hits a golden oak in other songs on his way to

Aušra's wedding. In Baltic folklore, the oak tree is linked to the thunder god. A source from the first part of the 1800s talks about the Lithuanian Perkūno Ġžuolas or the Latvian Pērkona Ozols.

Other stories say that Perkūnas would marry Laumė or Vaiva on Thursday. However, Velnias took the bride, and Perkūnas has been after Velnias ever since. Some stories talk about Perkūnas' four sons, who are said to be linked to the four seasons of the year or the four directions for the globe. There are seven and nine Perkūnai who are sometimes called brothers. "Perkūnų yra daug" is the Lithuanian phrase for it. Some stories say that Perkūnas sends his wife into the sky and stays alone. In some myths, the story is very different: Dievas pulls Perkūnas off the ground and into the sky. The idea behind Perkūnas's stones within the sky comes from Indo-European folklore. In Lithuanian, Perkūnkalnis means "mountain of Perkūnas", or Griausmo kalas means "mountain of rumble." Perkūnas live on high terrain or mountains.

One crucial thing that Perkūnas does is fight Velnias. He is the deity of the earth and death and is sometimes seen as the opposite of Perkūnas. "Velnias" is like the "devil" to Christians, but this is not how ancient people thought about them. In this story, Perkūnas goes after Velns because he stole fertility and cattle, which is called picaroon. Velnias lurks in trees and under rocks, or he can change into a black cat, a dog, a pig, a goat, a lamb, a pike, a cow, or a person. On a carriage made of stone and fire, Perkūnas chases an enemy through the sky. The wagon is sometimes made of red iron. It is pulled by two horses, one red and one white. Ratainyčia is the Lithuanian god of horses and chariots. It's a made-up picture of Didieji Grįžulo Ratai's chariot. In Samogitian art, Perkūnas is shown as a horseman riding a burning horse, which fits this. Perkūnas rides into town on his heaven chariot as an old man with grey hair and a big beard that is made up of many different colours. He wears white and black clothing and holds a goat on a cord with one hand while grasping a horn or an axe in the other.

Perkūnas has many tools. Some include a stick, lightning bolts, an axe and sledgehammer, rocks, a sword, an axe and sledgehammer, and an iron or fire knife. The weapons were either made by Perkūnas or with help from Televelis, the holy blacksmith from heaven. Something against Perkūnas hides in the hollow of a tree or a rock. A thunderstorm is the end of Perkūnas' search for his opponent. It eliminates any evil spirits and brings back any stolen stock or weapons. Thursday is also linked to Perkūnas. In many cultures, Thursday is the feast of the Thunderer. For example, in Poland, it's called Peraune-dįn, and in Lithuania, it's Perkūno diena.

In early sources, Perkūnas is linked to Jupiter, the Roman god. Tuesday through Thursday are stormy days with rain and thunder.

Velnias: God of the Underworld

Velnias' name is derived from the word vélé, which means a ghost of a dead person. Velnia's stories are some of the most well-known in Baltic tales. He was a deity of the dead, but trade, hunting, and farming were also linked to him. He was either an ally or an enemy of the sky god Dievas and worked closely with him. He looks much like the Germanic god Patula, the Scandinavian god Odin, and the Hindu gods Varuna and Vritra. Velnias is one of the most well-known characters in Lithuanian folklore, and he is talked about a lot in beliefs, myths, poems, and songs. After he learned about Christianity, his character changed to play the Christian devil.

As Velnias, he could change his appearance into many different shapes and sizes. Shape-shifting is a popular theme in Baltic folk tales. The velnias took the form of different birds, animals, and snakes. He was able to change into different people of all ages and jobs. Velnias had a complicated connection with people. He may want to be friends with them, love them, accept them, or give them help. He helped people work their land and build homes, churches, bridges, and farms. He helped people who needed it, like hunters and blacksmiths. He could also do different kinds of harm to people. Tempted them to sin, went into their souls and enticed them, made fun of and mocked them.

Velnias looked after the dead. He changed forms and returned to life as an animal, making him their protector god. He also looked out for farmers and herders. In folk tales, Velnias had been a handsome man who tried to win the love of women and, at times, even marry them. According to Christians, stories about Velnias's relationships with women were primarily false, which made his image even worse. In many different cultures and countries, the person who thinks has a helper who makes their thoughts come to life.

Most of the time, the helper doesn't want to do their job or is dishonest and causes problems. Velnias worked for the gods, but his story is about more than that. In the beginning of Baltic folklore, Velnias appears as one of the beings who created the universe and the material world. His link to death and rebirth goes back to ancient times and the worship of Baltic ancestors. The god of the abyss and the guardian of the dead was Velnias. Historical records also link him to farming, hunting, trade, and crafts. Depending on the story, he either works with Dievas as an enemy or as a helper in making the earth. Velnias looked out for the earth's and animals' growth and wealth.

After Christianity came to the area, Velnias changed some of his traits to those of the opposite of God, also known as the Devil or Satan. Folklore connects Velnias to the Christian devil, rendering him a famous character in stories. He shows up as different animals, birds, and snakes. He often has trouble getting along with other people. He sometimes looks for friends, love, or help. He aids them in many ways, like keeping them safe from evil people, building homes and roads, and working their land. He can also hurt people, make fun of them, trick them, tempt them to sin, and try to lure them. Velnias was a protector for the dead in myths from before Christianity. He looked out for animals and kept the farmers and herders safe. According to Lithuanian folklore, the deities are beings from heaven. Velnias was made to be the gods' triple on Earth, so his realm was in the abyss, and everything was the opposite of what happened on Earth.

CHAPTER 3: GODDESS

In mythology, goddesses are revered, often ethereal beings who play essential parts in the stories and spiritual beliefs of people worldwide. These holy female beings have unique traits ranging from caring and motherly to fierce and mysterious. Goddesses have stood for things like creation, fertility, wisdom, and protection in many countries and times.

They are revered as examples of the power and goodness of women, who shape fates, change the cycles of nature, and lead the way for people. In myths, legends, and religious stories, gods show us the many sides of being a woman, the mysteries of the universe, and the deep ties between humans and the divine. Myths about them often reflect societal ideals and ideas of what it means to be a woman, which gives us a glimpse into how men and women interacted in the past. This chapter explores mythology's fascinating world of goddesses, looking at their roles, traits, and meanings in different old cultures.

Veliona: Goddess of the dead

The dead were taken care of by Veliona. An important temple to the goddess Veliona was built on top of a church in Veliuona. Veliona is a Chthonic goddess who watches over the water, rocks, streams, and land. In Germanic mythology, Veliona played a part similar to that of the Valkyries. People thought that she took in the souls of soldiers who had died in battle. Traditional stories say that many pings were sacrificed to Veliona. There were also hens, roosters, female calves, and lambs.

Verona, also known as the "Dark Mother," is the goddess who watches over Earth, water, and places underground. She and her husband, Velinas, are in charge of the Veles, the souls of the dead in her underground realm. Her main job is to watch over the dead. Yet, she also watches over water, mainly underground water and secret treasure. Veliona rules over the productivity of people, animals, and land. So she can keep a watchful eye on her kids; she lives on Earth. In general, Veliona is the guardian of the dead. However, she especially lets fallen warriors enter her realms, especially people who died defending Lithuania from Christian crusaders.

A short story says that Veliona stopped the water flow and caused a drought. The thunder goddess Perkūnė then tried to find Veliona to kill her so the water could flow again. In another story, Veliona helps poor people by lending them money that she gets from her magic. Beings called vilutės, who live underground with Veliona, are sometimes given this job. However, they don't always do it or pay attention to people asking for money.

People thought the goddess and the souls living on the earth affected farming and animal health. To please her and the souls, they made unique gifts to Veliona. They scattered crumbled food over the land and dug some into the ground. On November 2, Vėlinės is honoured, and these small ceremonies are linked to it. They are meant to help you remember your deceased family members and give gifts to the goddess Veliona.

Velines is the Lithuanian holiday for the dead, and Veliona is responsible for it. Once upon a time, the event happened in October during harvest celebrations and went on for four weeks. Because of Christian impact, the holiday has been cut down to just one day, November 2, and the night before. People in some parts of Lithuania killed pigs during the holiday. Other animals, like cows, goats, sheep, and chickens, were also killed. The oldest family member made a sacrifice right away and gave it to Velinas. Then, portions meant for Veliona were cooked right away in a grain pot and served immediately. The souls of resurrected dead family members, the Veles, were also given food.

Goddess Gabija: Goddess of Fire

Gabija is the goddess of fire and home to the people of Lithuania. She keeps the home and family safe and brings happiness to children. Her name comes from the Greek word gaubti, which means St. Agatha. Jan Łasicki only wrote about Gabija in a list of Lithuanian gods, and she later appears in Lithuanian myth. Gabija could change into a cat, stork, rooster, or a woman dressed in red. People in Gabija treated fire with great respect as if it were a live thing. Gabija would eat bread and salt that people gave her. People had to put out fires at night. Women covered charcoal with ashes every night so the fire wouldn't move.

In the same way that Gabija watched over the house, mother for the house watched over the fire. She could occasionally wash herself by leaving a bowl of water safe beside the fire. Gabija would "take herself for a walk" and set the house on fire if she was mad. Much folklore says that people who insulted Gabija by pounding, spitting, or spitting on fire would have bad things happen to them.

This is Gabija, the Hearth Fire Goddess. All

ceremonies begin with gifts given to her. Women are the only ones who care for her, bring her gifts, and bank at night. She is just one of several goddesses for whom many rites are only for women. Gabija needs the same kind of care as Žemyna because she gives heat for food and warmth over the house. For Lithuanians, fire represented one of the most holy things in the world. Gabriela should always have clean water on its banks. People think anything dirty would get into Gabija's eyes and hurt her, so water must be as clean as possible. Gabija would burn down the house as a way to get back at someone who hurt her.

In the hearth, a fire will never go out; it's just put out for the night. The fire could only be put out once a year, during Rasa's or Jonines's time. On the Summer Solstice, the holy fire has to be brought from Lithuania's spiritual centre. The fire was moved around the farmland of Lithuania by long chains of people. Gabija's holy cult has roots in prehistoric times and is still going strong today. She has changed from being ornithomorphic to zoomorphic to humanomorphic. The word "Gabija" comes from the verb "apgaubti," which means "to hide." When Gabija sleeps, the coals and ashes are carefully stacked for the night, and prayers are said for her to "stay put" and not fall asleep. This was an essential job for the Lady of the Residence. In the past, she was given salt and food. "Gabija buk pasotinta" means "Gabija be full" if a piece of food or salt slips into the fire while the woman cooks.

The Home Fire is where all family ceremonies and acts of passage take place. Her presence is called for at the start of every routine, without which the rituals would not be possible. She agrees to take the offerings and talks to the other gods on their behalf. Gabija is unlike Vesta or Hestia, who are shy and quiet maiden aunts. Gabija is the most crucial part of every temple, grove, and house. Her flame represents everything that is truly alive. She is a powerful goddess who should be given the most tremendous respect. With more people, a group of women called Vaidelutės emerged as priestesses. The holy flame that lit for the "tauta" was cared for by them. They worked together to care for the fire and feed and comfort the Sacred Serpents while not having to do anything for their families.

She was also the Goddess of corn along with other grains as Gabjauja. When followers set up a meal or a fire, they give Gabija a gift. They would give beer for a meal, and for a fire, they would give water. Gabriela's fire kept thieves and demons out of the house, and only clean water could put it out. Gabija became linked to St. Agnes when Christianity came to the area. Some people spell her name Gabieta or Gabeta.Gabriela: Gabriela is the goddess of fire in the hearth. Women are the only ones who care for her, bring her gifts, and bank at night. She was among several goddesses for whom many practices are only done by women. The same goes for Gabija; she needs to be carefully cared for because she offers heat over cooking and warmth over the house. For Lithuanians, fire represented one of the most holy things in the world, and Gabija was surrounded by clean water. People thought that any dirt in the water would get into Gabija's eyes and hurt her, so it had to be as clean as possible. She would also burn down the house as a punishment if she were hurt.

The hearth fire would never go out; it would just go out for the night. During Rasa, the fire could only be put out once a year. The holy fire must be brought from the spiritual centre of Lithuania during the Rasa time. The fire was moved around the farmland of Lithuania by long chains of people—Goddess of the home hearth fire in Lithuania. During Rasa's time, women cared for the hearth and ensured it didn't go out more than once a year. They did this by making gifts to her, like throwing salt into the fire. Then, women would pick up a new fire at a holy centre and carry it from house to home across the country.

Every Baltic holiday has a fire going, whether on an altar, a bonfire, or a light. The most crucial thing in Lithuanian culture is fire. In the past, the Baltics were known for worshipping fire. The Eternal Flame was lit in the Sventaragis Valley, in the middle of Vilnius. Every home had a hearth that everyone in the family valued, but the mother took extra care of it and ensured it was safe. The fire meant more than just being a source of heat and light. In this case, it stood for the family's straight line of ancestors. The community's Eternal Flame brought together not only its living members but also its ancestors who had died long ago and were currently with the Gods. People thought that the centre of the fire was where many generations of the dead lived.

The word "Gabija" comes from the verb "apgaubti," which means "to hide." When Gabija sleeps, the coals and ashes are carefully stacked for the night, and prayers are said for her to "stay put" rather than roam. Every evening, this was an essential job for the mistress of the house. She would be meticulous and loving as she covered the coals with the prayers her mother had taught her. Forgetting to do this job or not being careful would ruin her home and the people she cared about because Gabija was never to be ignored or maltreated. You could take her "for a walk" and see how much damage she made when she was mad. Gabija is usually "fed" with salt and much food. "Gabija, be satisfied" is what the woman will say if some food or salt falls into the fire while cooking.

In your prayers, ask Gabija to stay put and live in us in peace. Saying "Bathe and recuperation, Fiery One" and leaving a bowl for freshwater by the fireplace is a common way to let Gabija know she is welcome to wash. Clean water is the only thing that will work when putting out the fire. Since fire has eyes, you can't put anything dirty into it. Much tradition says that people who spit or tread on her will have bad things happen to them. Carefully pick up loose coals and return them to the hearth and stove.

All family ceremonies and rights of passage took place around the hearth fire, run by a woman or male leader. They start every routine by asking her to be there because the rituals wouldn't be possible without her. She takes the offerings and talks to other gods and goddesses as a mediator. Many other Indo-European cultures have written about how she could heal, guard, and clean. This is not the shy, quiet, maiden aunt type like Vesta or Heslia. Gabija is essential in every building, grove, and home. She is the fiery representation of everything alive in that world. She is a goddess and a power that should be respected very much.

As the number of people increased, a group of priestesses called vaidilutes took care of the holy flame that burnt for the family, the tribe, and the whole country. At the start of February, there are a few days about the Goddess and the return of fire, the homestead gods waking up. The feast of Perkunas is on February 2. On this day, Visinski wrote about the traditions of the Samogitian people. A small beeswax candle called "perkunine" was wrapped around the piece of wood using a thick thread made of linen. All you have to do to make this kind of "wrapped candle" is wrap a linen thread around itself. It stands for life and the strength of the fire that never goes out. People light the Perkunas candle near a dying person or at a funeral to protect themselves from weather and other dangers.

Gabija Day is February 5. Gabija watches over the fire at home. Gabija's price for power is bread, salt, and water. To bless with fire, a "Perkunine" light is moved three times around the dining area and the stove. Next, a cross-shaped fire is held at the top, the back of the head, and underneath each ear to bless each family member. This is the sign of Perkunas. To do something like this is called "strengthening by fire."

Prayers to fire and fire rituals are performed on holidays and throughout the year. At the end of the year, two critical holidays, Kucios and Kaledos, mean that the world goes back to being dark and empty. But because death leads to birth, both holidays also mark the return of sunlight and the renewal of nature. The Lithuanians celebrate the next two days, now December 24th and 25th, with different rituals. In Indo-European societies, the New Year is celebrated with rituals and stories that reenact and talk about how the world was made. Folklore says that adults start getting ready for Kucios and Kaledos by putting a cherry branch in water on the first day of winter. Also, the day bears start to sleep. Just in preparation for the holiday, the twigs start to grow roots. Kids play games that are like planting crops. For example, girls can pretend to sow by spreading hemp seeds around the room, which makes them dream about future boyfriends.

People who are alive and people who are dead, as well as all living things, come together for the sombre feast of Kucios. The house needs to be prepared in a certain way. This is a famous "grove" that the family hangs up. It has birds made of wood, straw, or egg shells gathered around a straw sun. Many lit candles and this wood call to the spirits of the dead, who sit at a tiny table with Kucia, bread, and salt.

Along with nuts and honey water, the Kucia has many traditional foods for renewal, such as cooked wheat, barley, beans, peas, beans, rye, sunflower seeds, hemp seeds, and more. The Kucia gives food to both live people and the departed souls of the dead. The people who live there sit at a different table with hay and a tablecloth. In the past, hay was additionally utilized to cover the ground. The main table is decorated with signs of the vital force that keeps the world going. This includes a bag of rye that hasn't been thrashed yet. The family used this to wrap their apple trees the next day.

Kucios is a celebration that only happens at night. It starts when the last star shows up in the sky. Everyone takes a sauna bath, makes peace with their neighbours, and forgives their enemies before sitting down to the formal meal. In the past, the head of the family would walk around the farm three times while wearing tall black boots, a big black sash, and a big black hat. He would go to the front door after everyone else had come in. He replied, "Dearest God, because Kucia begs admission" to the question, "Who is there?"The oldest person in the family says a traditional prayer and breaks a Kucia bread, which everyone then gives to the next person. Praetorius, a historian from the 1600s, says that each household member put a loaf of food on the floor and prayed, "Zemepatis, bless you for the abundance of food you give us." Zemynele, please help us tend the fields and bless you so she will keep giving us good things. After that, everyone raised the loaf of bread to the heavens and said, "Feed us."

As the Kucia bread is passed around, each person drinks a beer and spills a few drops on the floor to honour the vele or souls who are dead. After that, dinner. Kucios used to need 13 distinct meals based on the 13 lunar years of the year. Since the solar clock was in charge, the number moved to 12. There can't be any dairy products or meat in the foods. Kucia, Kisielius, hot beet soup, onion dumplings, kale, fish, and seafood make up the meal. People and animals both eat the same food during the event. When humans and livestock lived together, everyone used the table to feed their pets and farm animals. On farms, people still feed the livestock Kucios that have been left over. Family groups also give food to fruit trees and bees.

Young people and children pull hay straws out from under the tablecloth after dinner while everyone stays there. A long straw means that you will live a long and happy life. There were also different ways for people to tell their fortunes. People make wishes for one another by putting grains into the fire in the hearth. The stove turns into the home's holy fire. If you plant a grain in the fire, it grows and does well. Every year, the family also burns a wood wreath, the stump, or wood in the fireplace to remember the old year. Participants can also eliminate evil by setting on fire splinters that have particular value to them.

CHAPTER 4: MYTHICAL CREATURES

In mythology, mythical animals are imaginary and often out-of-this-world beings that live in the worlds of imagination and folklore. These fascinating animals are a mix of human, animal, and supernatural parts that push the limits of the natural world. They are essential parts of the myths and legends of many different cultures. They have traits and symbols that show how complicated human feelings, fears, and hopes are. Mythical animals like dragons, tricksters, and good spirits capture our imaginations and help us share cultural knowledge, tell stories, and express ourselves through art. In different cultures, these creatures show how the human mind can think of anything and how beliefs make up a complex web that has changed societies throughout history.

But these animals have been discussed extensively in traditions, legends, fables, writing, mythology, fairy-tale novels, myths, and other types of fiction. People who believe in realism say that stories about magical creatures have existed long before history became a science. People have a lot of different views and ideas about mythical beasts, which leads to many different theories about whether or not they exist. This part shows a massive group of exciting mythical creatures that make you want to know more. Also, this article has some interesting facts about the argument over whether mythical creatures exist and some ideas about where these fantastical animals might have come from.

Zaltys: Household Spirit

Zaltys is a household spirit considered a part of the domestic environment and a sign of fertility in Lithuanian mythology. Zaltys is recognized as a household spirit. Many people believed it would bestow protection and good fortune upon them. As a pet of the goddess of the sun, Saule, people would keep it beside the stove or in a specific place in the house. This was because it was considered to be precious. People would try to make Zaltys feel more comfortable by feeding it milk if it was discovered in the field.

Sometimes, the family would invite the snake to join them at the table for supper. The family would suffer irreparable harm if the creature refused to comply. In the past, people believed that if they came upon a snake by mistake, it would be a perfect way to commemorate a birth and marriage. Those individuals who dared to take the life of the snake, which was considered to be the sentinel of the deities, would be in for a severe setback.

One of the species of grass snakes that are thought to be the Zaltys is the natrix tripodontus, which can be discovered in the forests or near individuals' homes. Those that are found coloured in the woods typically have a dark grey colour, whilst those that are found close to homes are typically green in colour. Because of its distinctive crescent-shaped head, the snake is easily distinguishable from other species of snakes.

Saule, the goddess of the sun, had a deep affection for all varieties of Zalciai and would frequently shed tears when she witnessed the death of one of them. It was believed that the red berries that were discovered on the mountains were symbolic of her weeping. In addition, it was stated that the snakes lounging in the sun were the reason for the connection between the two.

According to the beliefs of the Baltic people, the sun is a jar or jug filled with a golden fluid flowing out of it. Zalciai can take in the sun's beneficent and curative energy through their body, which allows them to live longer. Because it represents life and energy, the serpent Zaltys can never be destroyed. Zalktis was the name given to the Latvian form of the Zaltys. In contrast, Zalciai was given the plural form of the word Zaltys after it was pluralized.

As long as they are correctly cared for, individuals can have Zaltys within their domicile. As a result of the fact that these snakes are regarded as being harmless, they aren't thought of to be dangerous to humans. Once upon a time, people believed the best way to safeguard them was to keep them inside the house where children played. Even though keeping a Zaltys may bring its owner luck, the reasons for its protection are considerably more profound. It is believed that all of the family's ancestors are members of the Zaltys, which is an old belief. Additionally, the deity dubbed Pagirnis protects the family's wealth and the soil.

There is a widespread belief that the Zalciai are connected to the fertility of the earth and the advancement of agricultural production. Specifically, this is because both the World Tree and the Zaltys are connected to the development of crops. Moreover, they are well-versed in medicinal plants and herbs, and ladies would carry roasted snakes to protect themselves from illness.

The year 1387 marked the year that Lithuania became a Christian nation; nonetheless, the belief in the snake Zaltys remained to be maintained by the ordinary people. The practice of worshipping snakes, which dates back to prehistoric times and is still practised now, is said to have survived and is represented by this thought. Attaining a smooth amalgamation of ancient customs and contemporary Christian principles is a feat that the region's inhabitants have been able to do. The presence of characteristics specific to the region inside the framework of the modern belief system proves this.

Kaukas:Sprit of Harvest

Kaukas is a fertility, harvesting, and wealth being in Lithuanian mythology. He is also known as the Kaukas. Some names that refer to Kaukas are Kaukutis, Kukas, and Pūkis. Kaukai spirits can be male or female; nevertheless, men are more prevalent. The Kaukai were thought to either visit or remain in the homestead, where they kept a watchful eye on the people who lived there. There are rumours that Kaukai can be seen when the moonlight shines or fog in the air. The celebration that takes place every year in the spring and is now known as Mardi Gras was initially held in honour of the Kaukai spirits. The ceremony was under the direction of a masquerader known as "boba" or "mother." At the festival, the participants adorned themselves with masks known as "kaukės," dressed up as various animals, and adorned their heads with horns.

Aitvaras: Guardian of Water

In the mythology of Lithuania, Aitvaras is a celestial creation that belongs to the Pantheon of pagan deities. The ocean, the atmosphere, and the clouds are all under his protection. Aitvaras can bestow financial wealth upon people due to his relationship with the soil and the resources it contains. According to Baltic mythology, the Aitvaras is a flying dragon or rooster portrayed as either a spirit that brings good fortune or a spirit that is a trickster. Moreover, they are sometimes called minor demons, spirits of the home and the natural world. It is an unexpected monster that, depending on the area in which it is currently located, can shift into various forms. For example, it can appear to be a black cat and a black cockerel while staying in the house.

The Aitvaras are a sort of serpent with a head in the shape of a grass snake that is considered lucky. At any given moment, they can fly and transform into other shapes. These beasts were formidable monsters that roamed the wilds and lived in the woods. It is possible to convince them to take on the role of guardian or protector for the family. Their role as a guardian allows them to bestow prosperity and happiness upon anybody they choose. Before the advent of Christianity, their Aitvaras were considered to be semi-divine beings that could safeguard a family or individual household. Additionally, they were utilized to govern the wealth of individuals within their respective communities.

There are many different ways to describe Aitvaras as a species, among which is that they have the power to shift into various shapes. There are also instances of them appearing in various civilizations, typically in the form of a rooster, like a black cockerel that can be seen inside a house or a barn. They may emerge as black cats on other occasions. An Aitvaras can turn into a flying serpent or a burning snake when flying through the air. Additionally, it can become a comet or a rock when travelling through the air.

There are moments when Aitvaras is judged to be a reasonable creature, and there are other times when he is judged to be nasty. Without being asked, he maintains a covert operation. Aitvaras protect the righteous individuals whom others have harmed. He protects those who aren't greedy, and he bestows upon them a variety of wealth, including grain, flax, and money, typically stolen from wealthy individuals who are greedy. Once a person has gained the favour of Aitvaras, they will no longer be subjected to any further suffering; yet, the treasures that Aitvaras bring with them do not necessarily ensure that they will have a prosperous future.

There is a lack of information regarding the replication of Aitvaras. To produce one, an egg must be laid by either a rooster or a cockerel that is seven years old. Once the Aitvaras emerge, they are kept warm under the armpit till they emerge. There is a common belief that the Aitvaras consume the leftover food in their houses. However, they are most likely eating milk, eggs, and grain taken from animals in the surrounding area. Atvaras, Damavykas, Pūkis, Sparyžius, Gausinėlis, Žaltvikšas, and Spirukas are some of the other names that are used to refer to Aitvaras. It is worth noting that Aitvaras is entirely identical to the Latvian Pūķis. It is not quite crystal clear where the word "Aitvaras" originated from. Although some believe it originated from the term tverti, some claim it derived from the word aitauti.

There is both good and evil in the Aitvaras. They are capable of causing fires and destroying crops, yet they also can deliver wealth to humans. Even though their homes are brimming with beautiful things, most people are unaware they possess an Aitvara. People who are not greedy or abused by others are the ones that Aitvaras takes care of. It gives them a variety of fortune, including cereal, flax, and money, which they typically take away from people who are wealthy and selfish.

Additionally, Aitvaras can heal themselves by infusing themselves with the Earth. Despite this, some have been known to kill the creatures to eradicate them from their homes.

CHAPTER 5: LEGENDS

A legend is an old story or collection of stories about a person or place. The word "legend" meant a story about a holy person. According to legends, stories about supernatural beings, mythical creatures, or natural events are similar to folktales in what they say. However, legends are specific to a place or person and are told as historical facts.

Mythology studies stories that combine history, imagination, and traditional beliefs. These stories are called legends. In these stories, strange people, places, or things often cross the line between reality and the supernatural. Legends are told from generation to generation, becoming a big part of a community's identity and way of sharing stories. On the other hand, many local stories are just well-known stories linked to a specific person or place. Whether they are about heroic acts, the origins of natural landmarks, or the lives of famous people, these stories show what people value, what they hope for, and what makes life mysterious. Mythology's legends are a link between the every day and the extraordinary. They remind people of their past and show how people are the same across time and countries.

The concept of the Life after Death

In the Lithuanian myth of Sovijus, the horizon of death cuts the shapes of some of the most significant gods. Sovijus worshipped the dead foresters, who were worshipped by the main idols of Lithuanian custom. In the background of death, the group is writing down its rules. It looks like death wasn't seen as the terrible end of life; instead, it was likely seen as the expected end of life and its continuation in some other form.

As you can see, the journey of dead people begins with the fire that kills warriors and nobles. However, some beliefs that were still around not too long ago show that there is a gap in time between death and the time of entering the other world that causes the dead to stay in this world. It was thought that Dievas gave each person a certain number of years to live. If a person couldn't live the whole number of years—for example, if they perished, committed suicide, or died too soon—they had to stay on earth until their appointed date of death by changing into plants, usually trees, animals, or birds. Some people also thought that the dead could only leave this world once a year, on All Souls Easter, which is also known as Shrove Thursday. Another version of this story says that it was All Souls Day, and before that date, the dead had to stay on earth. Because of this, some individuals live on Earth. Because of Christianity, these souls became linked to sinners who were sorry and wanted to go to purgatory. As a result, purgatory was pulled closer to Earth. The old metempsychosis system helped people believe in these pictures. There are many examples of this system in the Lithuanian view of the afterlife. Let's say that the souls of the dead in hell have changed into working beasts and oxen that carry big loads. In other cases, the souls of the dead show up as a flock of sheep. In heaven, the dead can come back to life as birds.

The rock is the most important symbol of the afterlife because the God, or Perkūnas, lives on top of it. The home of the dead starts behind it or on top of it. It is bright and warm, with a beautiful yard with many birds singing. People sometimes think that the dead have to use their own or animals' nails to climb a hill after they die. At the base of the hill, there lives a snake. This is where the devil's space is, and it looks like hell is directly beneath the mountain, which means it's under the place where the dead live in heaven. The dead inhabit places where birds fly to spend the winter. The Milky Way helps the birds find their way. People may have considered the Milky Way a mythical cosmic mountain or its slope, which people had to climb and birds could fly to.

Neris and Nemunas

Neris, who was both nimble and happy, used to run between the green hills at one point. An eager young Neris made a beeline toward Dauguva. Nothing appeared to be able to change the direction she was heading. After that, however, she became aware of Nemunas. In addition, Neris decided one morning that she wanted to go in his direction. The hollow sound of the Earth echoed, "But you have to go to Dauguva," as a massive chain of hills obstructed her route. "But you have nowhere else to go."

Neris experienced a sense of unease. She had a strong desire to see Nemunas, but she could not ignore the Earth's wishes. She struggled and twisted as she was torn between the two options. Through this process, the Great and Little Svyruonėliai* settlements existed. Neris continued to feel depressed even though birds sang love songs. At this location, five islands and a big river loop next to Buivydžiai came into existence.

Last but not least, the Earth gave in. Neris's delight was inexhaustible; she flailed her arms and laughed out loud among the crowd. It was a joyful dance that took place. Today, people call this location the Shoal for the Dance of Virgins.

The hills and valleys along the shore were also happy, and Neris found new ways to travel through some of the most breathtaking locations. Several friends, including Žeimena, Vilnia, Vokė, Bražuolė, Žiežmara, and Musė, gathered around her in succession. Eventually, even the vast majority of Šventoji hurried to join them. Nemunas was the first thing that Neris saw when she opened her blue eyes, donned a white veil of fog, and looked forward to meeting her. Flowers blossomed in abundance at the point where both rivers met.

There was widespread dissemination of information on Nemunas and Neris and their trek to the sea together. When Nemunas and Neris arrived in Lithuania, the country's rivers came to meet them. They contributed water to these two magnificent rivers. The only one who was late was the stunning Minija of Semogitia. Nobody knows whether she travelled to the bay alone or the tremendous but persistent Nemunas guided her there. This is something that has not been determined to this day.

Printed in Great Britain
by Amazon